Blue French Bulldog

The Complete Owner's Manual

Care, costs, breeders, puppies for
sale, price, adoption, health,
training, all covered

Including facts for Miniature Blue French Bulldogs and
Black, Grey, White and Brindle French Bulldogs

Description

All information you need to know about Blue French Bulldogs.

Care, costs, breeders, puppies for sale, price, adoption, health, training, all included. The definitive guide for anybody passionate about Blue French Bulldogs. Includes facts and information for Miniature Blue French Bulldogs and Black, Grey, White and Brindle French Bulldogs.

Within the pages of this book, you will receive an in-depth look at the Blue French Bulldog breed as well as information on the different size and color options. The book covers everything, from finding a breeder and picking a puppy to feeding, grooming, and training your Blue Frenchie. You will also learn about common health problems, how to prevent them and many more topics.

This book is written in a clear and comprehensible fashion and covers all aspects of keeping and caring for a Blue French Bulldog. It is full of sound advice presented in an easy-to-read style and it is guaranteed to provide straightforward answers to all your questions.

Table of Contents

Introduction

With his big, bat-like ears and his goofy personality, the French Bulldog is a unique and wonderful breed. Though the breed was developed as a shopkeeper's companion, keeping the workroom free from rats, he has since become known as a loving family pet and a favorite among urban dwellers. Not only is this breed easy to care for, but his winning personality comes as a bonus.

As is true for many breeds, the French Bulldog comes in a wide range of colors and patterns. One of the most sought-after colors is blue. The Blue French Bulldog has a beautiful grey coat with a blueish sheen. Though the color of his coat definitely sets him apart, the Blue French Bulldog shares all of the other wonderful qualities that makes this breed so popular among singles and families alike. It is no wonder that this breed consistently ranks among the 15 most popular breeds in the United States!

Although the Blue French Bulldog is an exceptional breed by far, being a dog owner always comes with certain challenges. This breed is relatively easy to care for due to his short coat and low exercise needs, but he does require a great deal of attention and he may be stubborn sometimes when it comes to training. This, combined with the fact that a small dog like this can have up to a 15-year lifespan, means that you need to think carefully before you bring home a puppy, to determine whether it really is the best choice for you and for your family. Giving a puppy as a gift may seem like a good idea, but it is an important decision to think through.

Whether you have already decided on the Blue French Bulldog as your dog breed of choice, or you are simply hoping to learn more about these happy-go-lucky little dogs, you have come to the right place. Within the pages of this book, you will receive an in-depth look at the Blue French Bulldog as well as information on the different size and color options. We will cover everything from finding a breeder and picking a puppy to feeding, grooming, and training your Blue Frenchie. You will also learn about common health problems and how to prevent them.

By the time you finish reading this book, you will know everything you need to know to decide if this is the pet for you and for your family. If you decide it is, you will be well on your way to becoming the best dog owner you can be!

So, if you are ready to get started in discovering just what makes the Blue French Bulldog such a joy, simply turn the page and keep reading!

Chapter One: Intro to French Bulldogs

Though he may be small, the French Bulldog packs a lot of personality into a tiny package. This breed is tough on the outside but incredibly sweet on the inside, making him a wonderful family pet. Before getting into the details about the Blue French Bulldog in particular, you should learn the basics about the breed as a whole. In this chapter, you will find an overview of French Bulldog facts as well as detailed information about the breed's history. With this foundation of knowledge, you will be better equipped to understand what makes the Blue Frenchie so unique as you read the rest of this book.

1.) What is a French Bulldog?

The French Bulldog is a small-breed dog known for his compact size and friendly personality. Affectionately known as the "Frenchie," this breed is consistently ranked among the top 15 dog breeds in the United States, according to registration statistics with the American Kennel Club (AKC). What makes this breed so popular is the fact that he is easy to care for, he loves to spend time with people, and he is adaptable to different living situations.

The average size for the French Bulldog breed is about 16 to 28 pounds (7.3 to 12.7 kg) at maturity. Males of the breed are toward the higher end of the spectrum, weighing 20 to 28 pounds (9 to 12.7 kg), while females are toward the lower end, topping out at 16 to 24 pounds (7.25 to 11 kg). Though this may be one of the smaller dog breeds out there, Frenchies actually have a very strong and sturdy build. Their bodies are well-muscled, and they can accurately be described as "big boned".

Though the French Bulldog might not be as cute and fluffy as some other small-breed dogs, his winning personality more than makes up for any shortcomings with his appearance. Not only are these dogs incredibly friendly, but they absolutely adore people and they make wonderful companion pets. You will be hard-pressed to find a breed that is more loyal and affectionate than the Frenchie. Just keep in mind that he is more likely to make friends with strangers than to scare them away as a guard dog.

In terms of coat and coloration, the French Bulldog has a short, close-lying coat. The texture is smooth and fine and soft to the touch. Another characteristic that makes this breed unique is the folds of skin that cover his face and parts of his body. Coat colors typically include fawn, cream, or brindle, though other colorations are possible as well. Most dogs have dark eyes and a black nose as well as large, bat-like ears that stand erect. The tail is short and tapers to a point – it may also be either straight or screwed.

Although the Frenchie is a small-breed dog, his lifespan is a little shorter than other breeds of his size. These dogs usually live for 11 to 13 years, compared to the 12 to 15-year lifespan many small breeds achieve. This is partially due to the fact that Frenchies are a brachycephalic breed – this simply means that they have a pushed-in facial structure which can sometimes inhibit their breathing and may also contribute to health problems. The breed is also highly prone to obesity, which can lead to other serious diseases and significantly reduce your dog's lifespan. You will learn more about other health problems common in the breed later in this book.

French Bulldogs are lively little dogs, but their needs for exercise are only low to moderate. While your dog might be perfectly content to sleep on the couch all day, taking him for a daily walk is important for his health and wellness. You should be careful about subjecting your dog to vigorous exercise due to his breathing difficulties, but a brisk 20 to 30-minute walk once a day will be very good for his health. Working off his excess energy will also reduce the risk for problem behavior.

Caring for the French Bulldog is fairly straightforward. In addition to taking him on a daily walk and giving him plenty of love and attention, you will also need to feed him a high-quality diet and take care of his grooming needs. A small-breed dog food formula is ideal for the Frenchie – you will learn more about feeding your dog in a later chapter. In terms of grooming needs, the Frenchie's coat is easy to care for, but you will also have to trim his nails, clean his ears, and keep his wrinkles clean and dry.

When it comes to training, Frenchies are generally pretty good and they do have a desire to please their owners. Positive reinforcement training methods involving rewards for good behavior generally work the best for this breed – you will learn more about that later. Keep in mind that sometimes smaller breeds are more difficult to housetrain, but you can teach your dog to do pretty much anything with the right motivation and consistent training.

Summary of French Bulldog Facts

Breed Size: small

Height: 11 to 12 inches (28 to 30.5 cm)

Weight: 16 to 28 pounds (7.25 to 12.7 kg)

Coat Length: short

Coat Texture: fine and smooth; skin is soft and loose with wrinkles on the face, head, and shoulders

Accepted Colors: brindle, fawn, and cream (for AKC, UKC and The Kennel Club)

Other Colors: blue, solid black, mouse, liver, black and tan, black and white, and white with black

Eyes and Nose: eyes are dark in color and wideset; nose is black except in light-colored dogs

Ears: broad at the base, round top (bat ear); carried erect

Tail: short and either straight or screwed

Temperament: loving, playful, smart, clownish, lively

Strangers: quick to make friends, not inherently suspicious

Other Dogs: generally dog friendly

Other Pets: low prey drive

Training: smart with a strong desire to please; positive reinforcement training works well

Exercise Needs: moderately low; brisk daily walk

Health Conditions: hip dysplasia, allergies, patellar luxation, intervertebral disc disease, von Willebrand disease, elongated soft palate and brachycephalic syndrome

Lifespan: average 11 to 13 years

2.) French Bulldog History

The origin of the modern Frenchie can be traced back to the dogs kept by the Molossians, an ancient Greek tribe of people. Though the dogs were originally kept by the Greeks, it was Phoenician traders who spread them throughout the ancient world. Centuries ago, Molossian dogs were developed into what is now known as the Mastiff breed and then into a sub-family of Mastiffs known as the Bullenbeisser.

The Bullenbeisser breed was used almost exclusively for bull-baiting – a sport in which a dog was thrown into the ring with a bull tied to a stake. It was the dog's job to immobilize the bull, typically by grabbing hold of its nose and pinning it down. Blood sports like this were outlawed in England around 1835, which left bully breeds like the Bullenbeisser without a job. As a result, their use switched from being a sporting breed to being a companion breed.

To optimize the Bullenbeisser for companionship, the breed was bred down in size by crossing him with various terriers and other small breeds, such as the Pug. By the year 1850, the Toy Bulldog had become a popular breed in England and it had a strong following in the show ring. Dogs of this breed usually weighed between 16 and 25 pounds (7.3 to

11.3 kg), though there was also a class of dogs weighing less than 12 pounds (5.4 kg).

Around the same time that Toy Bulldogs were gaining popularity, the Industrial Revolution was taking place in France. Lace workers from the Nottingham area moved to Normandy, bringing with them a number of breeds including the Miniature Bulldog. As the breed became popular in France, interest in importing small Bulldogs increased. As a result, breeders in England began sending over their Bulldogs, which were considered too small as well as those that developed erect ears. Within ten years, the popularity of the Miniature Bulldog in France eclipsed the usefulness of the breed in England to the point that there were very few of them left in Britain at all.

As the popularity of smaller Bulldogs rose, they came to take on their own name – Bouledogue Francais. These dogs became highly fashionable and they were heavily sought after by Parisian society ladies– they were also popular among writers, artists, and fashion designers. Strict records of the breed's development were not kept, however, as it continued to diverge from its Miniature Bulldog roots. Crossings with Pugs and various terrier breeds reinforced some of the traits for which the modern French Bulldog is known, such as his erect ears and large, round eyes.

Not only did the French Bulldog rise in popularity in Europe, but it came to be very popular among society ladies in the United States too in the late 1800s. During the early 20th century, demand for the breed rose to the point where dogs were being sold for as much as $3,000 (£2,242) and they came to be owned by some of the most influential families in the United States, such as the J.P. Morgans and the Rockefellers. Very shortly after the breed club was formed, the French Bulldog was recognized by the AKC and, by 1906, it had become the fifth most popular breed in America.

Throughout its history, the French Bulldog exhibited a range of different colors, though black dogs were predominant. Today, some of the less common colors such as Blue French Bulldogs and Chocolate French Bulldogs have become known as rarities and they sell for higher prices than the more common colors. Currently, the French Bulldog ranks among the top 15 most popular breeds in America according to AKC registration statistics.

Chapter Two: Types of French Bulldogs

The French Bulldog is a friendly and loveable breed that makes a wonderful family pet. Even if you have already decided that the Frenchie is the right breed for you, you still have another decision to make — what kind of Frenchie do you want? Frenchies come in a wide range of different colors and patterns. They are even available in different sizes! In this chapter, you will learn the basics about French Bulldog genetics and you will be introduced to the different colors and sizes for the breed.

1.) French Bulldog Genetics

The French Bulldog is a pure breed which simply means that it is bred from two parents of the same variety rather than a mix of breeds. Purebred dogs inherit specific traits from their parents in keeping with the breed standard. This determines certain characteristics such as the breed's size, build, and temperament.

Though the basics of the French Bulldog breed are constant across the board, each litter of puppies will be slightly different due to the genetics of the parents. A Frenchie puppy inherits half of his genes from his mother and the other half from the father – the way these genes work in combination determines certain traits, such as the puppy's size, coat color, and even part of his temperament.

When it comes to coat color in dogs, there are only two basic pigments – black and red. Depending which of these pigments and how much each puppy inherits, the dog may exhibit a wide range of colors or patterns. For Frenchies, the primary colors are fawn, cream and brindle. Brindle is simply a coat that is patterned with streaks and specks of both light and dark-colored markings. The coat color and pattern of the parents will determine the coat color and pattern of the puppies.

2.) *French Bulldog Colors*

Now that you know a little bit more about how canine genetics works, you may be wondering exactly what colors you can expect to find within the French Bulldog breed. Again, the primary French Bulldog colors are fawn, cream and brindle. Within those colors, however, there are a lot of possible variations. Here is an overview of the different options for French Bulldog colors.

Fawn

This color ranges from light tan to a dark reddish tan as well as anything in between. Fawn French Bulldogs do not exhibit any brindle markings – they tend to be fairly uniform in color, though many dogs exhibit a dark mask on the eyes and muzzle. In order for a puppy to have a fawn coloration, he needs to inherit the fawn color gene from both the mother and the father.

Cream

Many fans of the French Bulldog breed consider the cream coloration to be simply a diluted fawn coloration. If you look at the genetics, however, you will find that the Cream

French Bulldog coloration is the result of two recessive genes. This color is usually a shade of eggshell white except in pied French Bulldogs, which may have an orangish tint to the overall fawn coloration. These dogs are sometimes called Beige French Bulldogs.

Brindle

The brindle coat is one that is predominantly dark in color with lighter hairs mixed in. The lighter hairs are sometimes mixed in a uniform pattern, but they can also be mixed in at random. The amount and concentration of lighter hairs comes with a specific name. For example, if the brindling is so subtle that it is almost non-existent, it is known as seal brindle. Tiger Brindle French Bulldog is very heavy brindling, or it may be a reverse brindle of dark hairs mixed in with a predominantly light-colored coat. The most common French Bulldog color overall is black brindle, though there are blue and chocolate brindles as well.

Black

Though many common French Bulldog colorations and patterns include some black, a solid black coloration is a little rarer. This coloration is only seen in dogs who have a recessive black gene from one of their parents.

Unfortunately, pure black Frenchies are not accepted by the AKC. There are other variations on the Black French Bulldog as well, such as black with tan points – this too is caused by a recessive gene. The reason black and blue Frenchies are excluded from AKC registration is because it was originally thought that the pure black coloration would dominate the other colors and overpower them. What is now known, however, is that the black gene is recessive, which makes the color fairly rare.

White

While the solid Black French Bulldog is fairly rare, many dogs of this breed exhibit white in their coloring. Solid White French Bulldogs are accepted by the AKC, as are dogs with brindle and white pattern. Dogs that are black and white or white with black markings are not accepted by the AKC.

Blue

Technically speaking, the Blue French Bulldog is a brindle coloration in which the predominant color is a slate-gray with a blueish sheen – this is why they are sometimes called Silver Blue French Bulldogs. Blue Brindle French Bulldogs are the result of a dilute gene inherited from both the mother and the father. The dilute gene causes the black hairs to take on a blue-gray hue and it also causes the pigment on the nose and foot pads to turn grayish blue as well. Eye color in the Blue French Bulldog is typically light to medium brown. Other color variations on the solid Blue French Bulldog are the Blue Pied French Bulldog, the Blue Fawn French Bulldog, and the Grey French Bulldog.

Grey

The Blue French Bulldog is sometimes called the Grey French Bulldog due to the similarities in the color. Depending exactly how much brindling the dog has, he may look more grey than blue, or vice versa.

Chocolate

The chocolate coloration for the French Bulldog is another brindle pattern and it can range in hue from a light milk chocolate color to a dark chocolate brown. Chocolate Brown French Bulldogs have brown noses and nails, but they can exhibit a wide range of eye colors including a lovely yellow-gold as well as light brown, hazel, or even green. Both this coloration and the blue coloration are fairly rare, so puppies with these colors tend to fetch a higher price.

Other Colors

Colors other than those described are also possible for the breed. For example, there are many Sable French Bulldogs as well as Lilac French Bulldogs. Red French Bulldogs are a little less common, but still a beautiful color. If you have your heart set on one of these French Bulldog colors, you will need to do some research to find a breeder. Generally speaking, however, it will be easier to find French Bulldog puppies in one of the more common colors mentioned above, than it is to find Blue French Bulldog puppies.

3.) Blue French Bulldog Sizes

The French Bulldog is generally classified as a small-breed dog, even though some dogs grow to more than 20 pounds (9 kg). The most common weight range for the French Bulldog full grown is 20 to 28 pounds (9 to 12.7 kg) for males and 16 to 24 pounds (7.25 to 11 kg) for females. The Blue French Bulldog exhibits this same weight range, because the genetics for size remain the same – only the genetics for color are different from the typical French Bulldog.

a.) Miniature Blue French Bulldogs

Though most Blue Frenchies weigh between 20 and 28 pounds (9 to 12.7 kg), there are some breeders who offer Miniature Blue French Bulldogs or teacup Blue French Bulldogs. These are not a separate breed – they are simply puppies that are selectively bred from smaller specimens of the Blue French Bulldog.

Miniature Blue French Bulldogs typically weigh 8 to 15 pounds (3.6 to 6.8 kg) full grown and Teacup Blue French Bulldogs weigh between 8 and 10 pounds (3.6 to 4.5 kg), depending on breeding. Generally speaking, the smaller the parent dogs, the smaller the pups will be.

Like their larger counterparts, Mini Blue French Bulldogs are friendly and very people-oriented. These little dogs are wonderful house pets, because they do not take up much space and they are largely content to spend the day lazing away on a warm lap. Miniature Blue French Bulldogs do well with children and they can also be friendly around other pets, provided you introduce them at an early age.

When it comes to the health and lifespan of Mini Blue French Bulldogs, there are no guarantees. Generally speaking, the Blue French Bulldog breed lives between 11 and 13 years. These dogs are affected by a number of health problems that can limit their lifespan and their laziness makes them highly prone to obesity. Miniature Blue French Bulldogs may have a higher risk for developing certain health problems than some of the larger sizes. For example, they are more prone to dental issues, due to their small skulls and they may have a higher risk for musculoskeletal conditions as well.

Caring for a Mini or Teacup Blue French Bulldog can be tricky for many reasons. For one thing, their small size makes them more fragile than larger Blue French Bulldogs – they may not be a good choice for very young children. Secondly, you need to be very careful about what you feed your dog – he needs enough protein to maintain a healthy bodyweight with enough fat to fuel his metabolism. You must walk the fine line, however, between overfeeding your Mini Blue French Bulldog and feeding him too little – a gain of even half a pound could be significant for a dog of this size.

Another challenge that is particularly common with Miniature or Teacup Blue French Bulldogs compared to the larger sizes is housetraining. Small and toy breeds are notorious for being a little difficult to housetrain, so the Mini Blue Frenchie might be as well. Though you cannot expect your puppy to be able to hold his bladder for too long at first, you should start teaching him good habits as soon as you bring him home. Always take him to the same spot in the yard when you take him out and supervise him closely when you are at home so he does not have an accident.

4.) Blue French Bulldog Mixes

In the world of dogs, designer dogs are becoming extremely popular. The term "designer dog" is often used for crossbreed mixes of two pure breeds. The first designer dogs were the Labradoodle and Goldendoodle – Poodles mixed with Labrador or Golden Retrievers. These dogs are known for their friendly personalities and their curly coats.

Technically speaking, it is possible to mix any two dog breeds together to create a new breed. You must be careful when breeding dogs, however, because some traits simply do not work well together. For example, if you bred a large-breed dog prone to joint problems (like the Great Dane) with a dwarf breed (like the Corgi), the resulting puppies would have a very high risk for bone and joint problems. This can also happen with health problems.

There is a theory called "hybrid vigor", which suggests that hybrids are healthier than purebreds due to a larger gene pool. In theory, this idea is sound but there is a great deal of controversy regarding whether it applies to designer dogs or not. Some breeds that have a very limited gene pool and a high risk for inherited conditions might benefit from an infusion of new blood. If, however, two breeds that are genetically predisposed to the same health problems are bred, the puppies have a much higher risk of getting it.

When it comes to Blue French Bulldog mixes, there are many possibilities. Generally, it works best to breed small dogs with small dogs, but that is not always what happens. Here is a list of some of the most common designer dogs made with the Blue French Bulldog breed:

- **Frug** – Blue French Bulldog and Pug
- **Frenchton** – Blue French Bulldog and Boston Terrier
- **Frengle** – Beagle and Blue French Bulldog
- **French Buillon** – Blue French Bulldog and Papillon
- **French Bull Dane** - Blue French Bulldog and Great Dane
- **French Bull Jack** - Blue French Bulldog and Jack Russel Terrier
- **French Bull Tzu** - Blue French Bulldog and Shih Tzu
- **French Bull Weiner** – Blue French Bulldog and Dachshund
- **French Pin** - Blue French Bulldog and Miniature Pinscher
- **Frenchie Bichon** - Blue French Bulldog and Bichon Frise
- **Frenchie-Pei** - Blue French Bulldog and Shar Pei
- **Frenchnese** - Blue French Bulldog and Havanese

If you like the Blue French Bulldog breed but you also like another breed, you might be able to get the best of both worlds by choosing a mixed breed. Before you choose, however, take a moment to think about some important facts associated with mixed breed dogs.

First and foremost, you must know that you cannot pick and choose which traits a mixed breed dog inherits. Many breeders claim that their designer dogs are the "best of both worlds", but the truth is that you cannot pick or control which traits are inherited from either parent. For example, unless the two breeds you pick to breed are the same size, you will not know until your Blue French Bulldog mix grows up how big he is going to be. Other traits such as personality and temperament can vary a lot in designer dogs, so keep that in mind as well.

If you have your heart set on a Miniature Blue French Bulldog or a Teacup Blue French Bulldog, you need to be very careful when speaking to breeders. There are some breeders out there who only want to make money and they will sometimes trick buyers by breeding a Blue French Bulldog with another toy or miniature breed to create a litter of extra-small puppies. If you are going to buy a Miniature Blue French Bulldog puppy from a breeder, be sure that you see both parents to ensure that the dog you are buying is actually a Blue French Bulldog and not a hybrid or mixed breed.

5.) *Blue French Bulldog Clothes*

Because Blue French Bulldogs are companion pets, many people who own them treat them more like children than like dogs. For example, Blue French Bulldog clothes are very popular. In some cases, clothes are used to express the dog's personality (or his owner's). Blue French Bulldog clothes can serve a practical purpose as well, however.

The Blue French Bulldog is prone to overheating due to his shortened facial structure, but his short coat may not provide enough protection during the winter if you live in a very cold place. Clothes like sweaters and jackets can help to keep your Blue Frenchie warm and comfortable. You might also consider buying your dog some booties to keep his feet warm in the winter. Dog booties can also protect the pads of his feet against rock salt and chemical-based ice melt products people use to keep their sidewalks clear of snow and ice during the winter.

Chapter Three: Practical Information for Owning a Blue French Bulldog

As wonderful as the Blue French Bulldog is, it is important to realize that owning a dog comes with certain responsibilities. If you choose to bring home a dog, you need to be prepared to care for that dog for the rest of his life. Before you make your choice, take the time to learn some practical information about keeping a dog, so you know whether or not it is really the best choice for you and for your family.

In this chapter, you will receive an overview of the practical aspects of keeping a Blue French Bulldog. You will learn about licensing your dog as well as important information about keeping this breed with other dogs and pets. You will also receive a list of pros and cons for the breed as well as an overview of the costs for keeping a Blue Frenchie as a pet. So, dive in and really take this information to heart!

1.) Do You Need a License?

Before you bring home a new pet, you need to make sure that it is legal to do so. This is primarily a concern with exotic pets, not so much with dogs, but there could be certain restrictions or regulations in your area that limit the size or type of dog you are allowed to keep. If you rent your home or apartment, it is even more important that you make sure there are no rules against dogs as pets – the last thing you want is to bring home a new puppy just to find out that you are not allowed to keep him.

Housing restrictions aside, it is legal to keep a dog as a pet in both the United States and the United Kingdom. There are, however, rules about licensing your dog that you need to understand. Generally speaking, you will be required to license your Blue French Bulldog if you live in the United

States. The specific rules about licensing dogs are set at the state level, however, so you should familiarize yourself with your state's regulations just to make sure.

When it comes to licensing your Blue French Bulldog in the United States, you will find that the license itself is rather easy to obtain and it generally costs less than $25 (£18.70). You will need to fill out a form with your name and contact information as well as information about your dog – his name, age, size, and breed. You may also be required to provide proof of an up-to-date rabies vaccination (rabies is a deadly viral disease spread by infected animals). Dog licenses generally last for 1 year and need to be renewed annually. Also, you will need to check with your state to see at what age you are required to license your dog – some states require puppies over the age of 3 months to be licensed, while others give you a full six months.

When it comes to licensing requirements in the United Kingdom, things are a little different than they are in the United States. In the United Kingdom, it is mandatory for all dog owners to license their dogs, so you will definitely need to get your Blue French Bulldog licensed if you live in the UK. Fortunately, the process is very simple and the cost is similar to a dog license in the U.S. You will also be glad to know that there aren't any vaccination requirements to obtain a dog license, because rabies has been eradicated from the UK. The only thing you might need to worry about is obtaining an Animal Movement License (AML) if you plan to purchase a puppy from outside the UK and bring him into the country.

2.) How Many Blue French Bulldogs Should You Get?

Because the Blue French Bulldog is such a friendly and fun-loving breed, you might be considering getting more than one. Having two dogs means that they will be able to keep each other company when you are away from home. This can be very important for a people-oriented breed like the Blue Frenchie. Unfortunately, not all Blue Frenchies get along with other dogs – even if they are of the same breed.

The first thing to think about before you bring home more than one Blue French Bulldog is whether you have the resources and space to care for two dogs. Though Blue Frenchies are not overly active and they remain fairly small, all dogs need a certain amount of space. If you live in a very small apartment or flat, having two dogs simply may not be practical for you. If you tend to spend a lot of time away from home, finding daytime care for two dogs may be more difficult than for one.

Aside from the practical aspects of keeping more than one Blue French Bulldog, you also have to think about whether the dog will get along with other dogs. Every dog is unique in terms of temperament and personality, but generally speaking, Blue Frenchies are not always the most dog-friendly of breeds. You are most likely to encounter problems if you keep two male Blue Frenchies together, especially if they are unaltered (not neutered). If you are able to raise two Blue Frenchies together as puppies, however, they have a better chance of getting along when they grow up.

Another thing to consider when keeping more than one dog is whether you have the time to give each of them the attention and love they deserve. Blue French Bulldogs tend to bond very closely with their owners and they can become jealous if you spend too much time with another pet – especially another dog. If you plan to keep two Blue Frenchies, make sure you give each of them plenty of individualized attention as well as spending time with both of them together when you are at home.

3.) Do Blue Frenchies Get Along with Other Pets?

Blue French Bulldogs are generally a peaceful and gentle breed. If you have other pets in the house already, however, you may want to exercise caution before adding another pet into the mix. Most Blue Frenchies get along well enough with other pets, but you really have to raise him from a puppy for the best results. You would also be wise to supervise all interactions between your dog and other pets, just to be safe. You never know how your pets are going to act around a dog and vice versa.

4.) *Blue French Bulldog Price and Costs*

When it comes to deciding whether the Blue French Bulldog is the right pet for you, you need to consider the costs. Owning a dog is not a small investment and it does come with certain monthly financial commitments. Keep reading to receive an overview of the costs associated with buying and keeping a Blue French Bulldog.

a.) Upfront Costs for Blue French Bulldogs

The upfront costs for keeping a Blue French Bulldog include the purchase price of the puppy, the cost of buying a crate and/or a dog bed, costs for food and water bowls, toys and accessories, microchipping, vaccinations, spay/neuter surgery, and grooming supplies. You will find an overview and an estimate of each of these costs for your Blue French Bulldog in the following pages:

Purchase Price for Blue French Bulldogs – The largest upfront price for your Blue Frenchie will be buying a puppy. Generally speaking, French Bulldog puppies usually sell for between $1400 and $2000 (£1050 - £1500).

You need to remember, however, that the Blue French Bulldog price will be higher. Blue is a rare color so puppies are likely to cost between $2000 and $4000 (£1500 - £3000). If you do not have your heart set on a puppy, you may be able to save some money by adopting an adult dog from a rescue. Adopted dogs usually go for between $100 and $200 (£75 - £150), though you may have a hard time finding a Blue French Bulldog through a rescue.

Dog Crate and/or Dog Bed – Once you bring your Blue French Bulldog home, you will need a place to keep him overnight and when you are away from home. Because this breed remains fairly small, you probably will not need to purchase a puppy crate and a separate adult crate. The average cost for a small crate and dog bed should be somewhere in the range of $50 to $100 (£38 - £75).

Food and Water Bowls – Again, because the Blue French Bulldog remains fairly small, you will only need to purchase one set of food and water bowls. You can save money by purchasing plastic bowls, but ceramic or stainless-steel bowls will be much more durable. Plus, they're easy to clean and less likely to harbor bacteria. Plan to spend about $20 (£15) on a set of nice dog bowls.

Toys and Accessories – When you first bring your dog home, you will want to provide him with an assortment of different toys, so you can learn what he likes. You will also need to purchase a collar, leash, and dog tags. The price range for these toys and accessories will probably be somewhere around $50 (£38).

Microchipping – Having your dog microchipped is not a requirement, but it is a very good idea. You will probably put a dog tag on your Blue French Bulldog's collar with his name and your contact information, but what happens if he gets out without his collar? A microchip is embedded under your dog's skin in a painless procedure and it provides a lifetime of protection. Each microchip has a specific number that will be linked to your contact information. So, as long as you keep the information updated, anyone who finds your dog if he gets lost will be able to take him to a shelter, have the microchip scanned, and then contact you. This procedure only costs about $30 (£22.50).

Vaccinations – If you are bringing home a Blue French Bulldog puppy, you will need to make sure he gets all of the necessary vaccinations at the right times. Your vet will tell you which vaccines he needs and when, but you should budget a cost of about $50 to $100 (£38 - £75) for puppy vaccines.

Grooming Supplies – In addition to toys and accessories, you will need certain grooming supplies to care for your Blue French Bulldog. Because his coat is short and smooth, a medium bristle brush or wire-pin brush will be adequate. You will also need a set of dog toenail clippers, some ear cleaning solution, and some wet wipes. The wipes are for your dog's skin folds – you will need to keep them clean and dry to prevent infection. The total cost for these things should be around $50 (£38).

Upfront Costs for Blue French Bulldogs	
Description of Cost	**Estimated Cost**
Purchase Price	$100 to $4000 (£75 - £3000)
Crate and/or Dog Bed	$50 to $100 (£38 - £75)
Food and Water Bowls	$20 (£15)
Toys and Accessories	$50 (£38)

Microchipping	$30 (£22.50)
Vaccinations	$50 to $100 (£38 - £75)
Spay or Neuter Surgery	$50 to $200 (£38 - £150)
Grooming Supplies	$50 (£38)
Total	$400 to $4550 (£300 – £3410)

b.) Monthly Costs for Blue French Bulldogs

In addition to considering the upfront costs for keeping a Blue French Bulldog, you also have to make sure you can cover certain monthly costs. These may include the cost of food and treats, veterinary care, license renewal, grooming costs, and replacements for toys and accessories. You will find an overview of each of these monthly costs as well as an estimate for each cost below:

Food and Treats – Because the Blue French Bulldog is a small breed, your monthly costs for food shouldn't be too high. You can expect to spend about $30 (£22.50) on a large bag of high-quality dog food that will last you about a month at a time. If you add on a bag of treats once a month, you are probably looking at $35 (£26).

Veterinary Care – Once your Blue French Bulldog puppy gets all the shots he needs during his first year, you will only need to take him to the vet every six months for check-ups. The average cost for a veterinary check-up is about $45 (£34). If you have two vet visits per year and you divide that total cost over 12 months, you will get a monthly cost of about $7.50 (£5.60).

License Renewal – Renewing your dog's license each year will not be a major expense – it should only cost you about $25 (£19). If you divide that cost over the course of twelve months you are left with a monthly cost of just $2 (£1.50).

Grooming – Because the Blue French Bulldog has a short coat, you probably will not need to have him professionally groomed very often. You will need to brush your dog's coat several times a week yourself, but monthly grooming is not necessary. If you do want to have him bathed and brushed out, it shouldn't cost more than $35 (£26), and you will only need to do it two or three times per year. Two grooming visits per year divided over twelve months is a monthly cost of around $6 (£4.50).

Other Costs – In addition to the costs that have already been mentioned, you may find yourself dealing with unexpected costs for the replacement of toys and food bowls, or you might need to replace your Blue French Bulldog's collar when he gets bigger. These costs will not occur every month, but you should set aside about $10 (£7.50) each month just to be prepared.

Monthly Costs for Blue French Bulldogs	
Description of Cost	**Estimated Cost**
Food and Treats	$35 (£26)
Vet Visits (2 per year)	$7.50 (£5.60)
Annual License Renewal	$2 (£1.50)
Grooming (3 per year)	$6 (£4.50)
Other Costs	$10 (£7.50)
Total	$60.50 (£45)

5.) Blue French Bulldog Pros and Cons

In addition to making sure that you can cover the cost of buying and keeping a Blue French Bulldog, you should also consider the pros and cons for the breed. These dogs make wonderful family pets, but there are some downsides to think about. Here is an overview of the pros and cons for keeping a Blue Frenchie as a pet:

Blue French Bulldog Pros:

- Remains fairly small (maximum 28 pounds, 12.7 kg), which is good for apartment or flat life.
- Has moderately low exercise requirements.
- Grooming is very easy, only needs to be brushed a few times a week.
- Small size means lower food costs than large dogs.
- Breed is generally good with other dogs and may get along with other pets when raised together.
- Friendly with strangers and can be good with kids.
- Bonds closely with family and loves to play.

Blue French Bulldog Cons:

- Blue color may be more difficult to find.
- As a rare color, Blue French Bulldogs can cost upwards of $2000.
- Shortened facial structure may cause breathing difficulties and could reduce lifespan.
- Can sometimes be stubborn or tricky to housebreak.
- May require more vet visits than other breeds due to potential health problems.
- Can sometimes be unfriendly with other dogs, especially other male dogs.

With these pros and cons in mind, as well as the other information from this chapter, you should have a pretty good idea whether this is the breed for you. If you are still not sure, however, you will find plenty more information in the rest of the book. So, keep reading!

Chapter Four: Blue French Bulldog Puppies and Where to Find Them for Sale

By now you should have a pretty good idea whether the Blue Frenchie is the right pet for you. If so, you may be wondering where to find Blue French Bulldog puppies or Blue French Bulldog breeders. In this chapter, you will receive tips for both. Not only that, but you will receive tips for picking a healthy puppy from a litter, as well as important information about adopting a Blue French Bulldog, if that is the route you choose to take.

1.) *Where to Find a Blue French Bulldog Breeder*

If you have your heart set on a Blue French Bulldog, your next step is to start looking around for Blue Frenchie puppies. You may be able to find a puppy at your local pet store, but think carefully about whether this is really the best option. Pet stores often get their puppies from puppy mills (rather than breeders) and they do not always come with a health guarantee. Some pet stores get their puppies and dogs from rescues, but that makes it even less likely for them to have Blue French Bulldog puppies for sale.

To find solid Blue French Bulldog puppies for sale, you will need to do some research. Start by doing some research online to find out if there is a Blue French Bulldog rescue nearby or if there is a breeder in your region. You should be prepared to travel a bit to get your puppy, though you may luck out and find a breeder close by. If that does not work, try asking around at your vet's office or talk to someone at a local shelter or pet store.

You will learn more about Blue French Bulldog adoption later in this chapter, but let's talk a little more about how to choose from different Blue French Bulldog breeders. Even if you find a breeder, you shouldn't stop your search – you should compile a list of several breeders and vet them all to choose the best one. As you do your research, be sure to view each breeder's website and make sure they are members of a breed club and that their breeding stock is certified and registered. If you do not plan to breed or show your Frenchie, this may be less important.

Once you have your list and you have reviewed the website for each breeder, take the time to call each of them on the phone. You will want to learn as much as you can from each breeder to make the best choice. Here are some questions to ask Blue French Bulldog breeders:

- How long have you been breeding Blue French Bulldogs?
- How do you select your breeding stock?
- Do you specialize in Blue French Bulldog puppies?
- Is your breeding stock certified, registered, and DNA-tested?
- What is your policy for reserving a puppy?
- What kind of health guarantee do you offer?

In addition to asking the breeder these questions, you should also see if they ask you questions back. A responsible breeder will take the time to get to know you to see if you are a good fit for one of their puppies. If you are looking specifically for Miniature Blue French Bulldog puppies for sale, make sure that the parents are still

purebred Frenchies – you do not want to pay good money
for a Mini Blue French Bulldog just to find out that it isn't a
purebred. It is always hard to tell with a baby Blue French
Bulldog exactly how big he will get – this is why it is so
important to see the parents before you buy a puppy.

2.) *How to Choose a Blue French Bulldog Puppy*

Once you have narrowed down your list of breeders and you feel ready to buy a Blue French Bulldog, you should pay a visit to the breeder of your choice. When you are faced with a whole litter of adorable Blue French Bulldog puppies for sale it is easy to get caught up in the excitement. If you want to ensure that the puppy you bring home is in good health, however, you will need to take your time with the decision.

When you visit the breeder, pay close attention to your surroundings and ask for a tour. You will want to see the parents and where they are kept, as well as the conditions in which the puppies are kept. If a breeder offers you a Blue French Bulldog puppy for sale but will not let you see the parents, it is a bad sign.

If, after your tour, you are pleased with what you see, you can move on to picking out your puppy. Here are some things to do to make sure you pick out a Blue Frenchie puppy that is healthy and well-bred:

- Take some time to watch the puppies and how they interact with each other – make sure they are active, not lethargic.

- Watch how the puppies react to your presence – they might be a little wary at first, but they should not be overly frightened, and they should get curious enough to approach you before too long.
- Kneel down and let the puppies come to you – interact with each one by petting them gently and speaking to them, watching to ensure they have a good response.
- Pick up the Blue French Bulldog puppies one by one to see what their temperament is like and to check for physical signs of illness or injury.
- Examine the Blue Frenchie puppies one-by-one to make sure they are in good health . A healthy puppy will display the following signs:
  - Clear, round, bright eyes with no sign of redness or discharge.
  - Clean ears – no redness, swelling, or odor.
  - No sign of diarrhea under the tail or in the puppies' living area.
  - Clean, soft fur with no patches missing, even in texture and length.
  - No bumps or visible wounds on the body.
  - Healthy activity and sound movement.

Once you have narrowed down your choices, ask the breeder for the veterinary and medical information for whatever puppy you are considering, to confirm that it is in good health. If the breeder requires a deposit to hold the puppy until he's ready to go home, ask about that. You should also ask about any health guarantees the breeder might offer. Never take home a puppy less than 8 weeks old – they need to be fully weaned before they go to their new homes. To make sure your puppy is weaned, try to schedule your visit around feeding time so you can watch the puppies eat to make sure they have a healthy appetite and that they have been fully transitioned onto solid food.

3.) *Blue French Bulldog Adoption Information*

Having a puppy is great, but it is also a lot of work! If you want to save some money and the hassle of dealing with the "puppy stage" with your Blue Frenchie, you might want to look into Blue French Bulldog adoption. Millions of pets end up in shelters each year and, sadly, many of them never find a new home. Adopting a dog could mean that you are literally saving a life and shelter dogs have a way of knowing that they have been rescued and they will be forever grateful to you for it.

Another benefit of adopting a dog is that you will not spend anything close to the typical Blue French Bulldog price range. Solid Blue French Bulldog puppies for sale can cost upwards of $2,000 (£1,495), but adopting a dog from a shelter will probably cost you less than $200 (£150). You might have to wait longer to find a Blue French Bulldog rather than one of the other colors, but it is possible to do it this way.

If you decide that Blue French Bulldog adoption is the right choice for you, you should be prepared to welcome a shelter dog into your home. Many dogs that end up in the shelter system have been neglected or abused, so they may come with certain health or behavioral problems. Even if the dog comes from a loving home, however, he could still be traumatized by the stress of being in the shelter. Many dogs in the shelter are subdued, even frightened. Once you get them home, however, their personalities start to come out and they may not always be good.

To ensure that your adopted Blue Frenchie is a good fit for your family, you might ask the shelter if you can foster him for a week or two before finalizing the adoption. This will give both of you a chance to get to know each other and you will have a better idea of what the dog is actually like. If you decide to adopt him, make him feel at home by creating a safe space somewhere in the house with his crate and bed as well as plenty of toys to play with. Do not force him to play or interact during the first few days until he is ready to do so, but show him lots of love!

Chapter Five: Blue French Bulldog Care

As a dog owner, it is your responsibility to make sure that your Blue French Bulldog's needs are taken care of. It all starts with prepping your home for a new puppy by puppy-proofing to keep your puppy safe. Next, you will need to learn what to feed your puppy and when to transition him to an adult dog food formula. You will also need to take care of your dog's grooming requirements. In this chapter, you will find a wealth of information about these three topics, so keep reading!

1.) *Blue French Bulldog Home Requirements*

The Blue French Bulldog is a small-breed dog, so he does not need a lot of space. These dogs are also highly adaptable, so your pup is likely to be just as happy in a large house as he is in a small flat – as long as you are there with him. You do not necessarily need a fenced yard, either, as long as you take your dog for a walk at least once a day and you play with him indoors to work off any excess energy.

When it comes to preparing your home for a new Blue Frenchie, you will need to do some puppy-proofing. Start by walking through your home and try to view it through a puppy's eyes to identify potential dangers. Here's a list of some of the things you may need to do:

- Store cleaning products where your puppy cannot reach them or put them in a locked cabinet.
- Put all trash in a can with a tight-fitting lid or keep it secured in a cupboard.
- Store open food containers in your pantry or cupboards – anything left out needs a lid.
- Tie up or bundle any electrical cords and blind cords so your puppy cannot chew on them.
- Pick up small objects from the floor – they are a choking hazard for dogs.

- Cover open bodies of water (such as the toilet, bathtub, outdoor ponds, etc.).
- Put all medications and other toiletries where your puppy cannot reach them, such as in the medicine cabinet and use child-proof bottles.
- Make sure none your houseplants or plants in your yard are toxic to dogs – if there are any, remove them, move them out of reach, or fence them off.
- Keep your windows and doors securely closed when your puppy is out – use baby gates or pet gates to keep him away from areas where you do not want him.
- If you have a cat, keep the litter box where your puppy cannot reach it, so he does not eat the clumps.
- Dispose of all food waste properly so your puppy cannot get it – this is especially important for chicken bones and foods that are harmful to dogs.
- Store all lawn and garden tools where your puppy cannot get to them and make sure they will not fall over if your puppy bumps into them.
- If you have a yard, consider adding a fence to keep your puppy in.
- Avoid using chemical fertilizers, pesticides, or herbicides where your puppy could be exposed.

Once you have puppy-proofed your home, the next step is to set up your puppy's area. You can choose a small room or use a puppy playpen to cordon off a section of a larger room. Place your puppy's crate and dog bed in the area as well as his food and water bowls and his treats. You will want to put your puppy in this area when you cannot actively watch him so he is less likely to get into trouble. While your puppy is very young, you will need to confine him to his crate until he is housetrained. You will learn more about that in a later chapter of this book.

2.) *Blue Frenchie Feeding Guide*

Many dog owners underestimate the importance of feeding their dog a high-quality dog food and they make the mistake of shopping for dog food by price alone. The problem with this method is that the cheaper the dog food is, the poorer the quality. Inexpensive dog food brands use low-quality fillers and other ingredients to add bulk to the product, but these ingredients do not usually provide any nutritional benefit. Without a healthy, high-quality diet, your Blue French Bulldog may not live as long as he could and he may develop other health problems.

a.) Nutritional Needs for Blue French Bulldogs

Before you go shopping for dog food, you should take the time to learn the basics about your Blue Frenchie's nutritional needs. Dogs are primarily carnivorous animals, so most of their nutrition needs should come from animal sources – things like meat, fish, and eggs. Your dog needs a balance of protein and fat in his diet, plus carbohydrates can provide energy, fiber, and other essential nutrients. It is important that your dog's food provides for his basic nutritional needs, because that is what he will be eating most of the time.

If you want to get into the specifics, know that protein is the most important nutrient for a dog. For Blue French Bulldog puppies, protein is required for healthy growth and development. When your puppy grows up, protein will help him maintain his lean muscle mass, so he does not become overweight or obese. Your puppy needs at least 22% protein in his diet and an adult dog needs 18%.

Next to protein, the most important nutrient for dogs is fat. While you may think of fat as a bad thing, it is an essential part of a balanced diet for dogs. Fat provides a concentrated source of energy and it helps your dog absorb and utilize fat-soluble vitamins. Fat should come from healthy animal sources like chicken fat or salmon oil and it should make up at least 8% of his diet. When he's an adult, he'll only need a minimum of 5%.

Technically speaking, dogs do not have specific requirements for carbohydrate in their diet. Carbs can provide energy and they contain fiber as well as other nutrients. What you need to remember is that your dog's body is not optimized for digesting and absorbing nutrition from plant products as much as from animal products, so any carbs in your dog's diet should be limited. They should also come from easily digestible sources like whole grains, starchy vegetables, beans, or legumes.

b.) Choosing a High-Quality Dog Food Brand

When shopping for dog food for your Blue French Bulldog, you need to read the information on the package to determine the quality of the product. If you are going to make a comparison between two different products, there are three specific things to look for on the label. First, look for the AAFCO statement of nutritional adequacy. If you are in the UK, check for information from the Food Standards Agency (FSA).

AAFCO is the Association of American Feed Control Officials and it is an organization that sets and upholds standards for pet food and animal feed. Before a product hits the shelf, they examine it to make sure it meets the minimum nutritional requirements for the intended animal which, in this case, is your dog. If the product is nutritionally balanced for dogs, you will see a statement like this somewhere on the label:

"[Product Name] is formulated to meet the nutritional levels established by the AAFCO Dog Food Nutrient Profiles."

If you see this on the package, you can rest assured that it will meet your dog's nutritional needs. Keep in mind, however, that the AAFCO statement does not guarantee quality – you still have to look at other parts of the package to determine whether the product is any good or not. After the AAFCO statement, look at the guaranteed analysis – this tells you the percentages of protein, fat, fiber, and moisture in the product. You can use the guaranteed analysis to make a direct comparison between two products using those minimum values from the last section. Because your dog is better able to digest meat than plant foods, try to keep the fiber content under 5%.

After checking the guaranteed analysis, the final place to look is the ingredients list. The ingredients list is ordered in descending order by volume, so the ingredients at the top are used in the highest quantity – this is the same for packages of food that you eat. You will want to see healthy, high-quality ingredients at the beginning of the list starting with a source of animal protein. Because dogs are carnivores, their bodies are better able to digest and absorb nutrition from animal sources. Quality sources of animal protein for dogs include poultry, meat, and seafood.

Aside from proteins, fats, and carbohydrates, there are some other beneficial ingredients you can look for. Supplemental vitamins and minerals are good because they help to ensure that your dog's specific nutritional needs are met. Keep in mind, however, that synthetic supplements are not as good for your dog as natural sources for the same nutrients – things like fresh fruits and vegetables. When it comes to mineral supplements, chelated minerals are ideal –

these are minerals that have been bound to protein molecules which makes them easier for your dog's body to utilize. If you see "dried fermentation products" on the list, do not be alarmed – these are probiotics that can support your dog's digestion.

c.) Tips for Feeding Your Blue French Bulldog

If you aren't sure what to feed your Blue French Bulldog, a small-breed recipe is a great place to start. On average, dogs need about 30 calories per pound (14 calories per kg) of bodyweight to sustain their metabolism each day. Larger dogs have slower metabolisms, however, and may only need 20 or 25 calories per pound (9 to 11 calories per kg). Small breeds like the Blue Frenchie, on the other hand, have very fast metabolisms and need more calories – up to 40 calories per pound (18 calories per kg) of bodyweight.

Small-breed dog food formulas tend to be higher in calories which will help meet your dog's energy needs. These recipes are usually higher in fat to achieve that higher calorie count, but you still need to make sure there is plenty of protein. When your Blue French Bulldog is young, feed him a small-breed puppy recipe and divide his daily portion into three meals. When he reaches about 75% of his maximum expected size, you can switch him over to a small-breed adult recipe.

Any time you change your Blue Frenchie's diet, be sure to mix a little of the old food with the new food to transition him slowly – this will help to prevent digestive upset. If you mix your dog's food properly and he is still having digestive issues, it could be something else – like food allergies. Food allergies affect dogs in a different way than they affect humans. While you might feel nauseous or sick after eating something you are allergic to, your dog will be more likely to develop skin problems. Red, itchy, and inflamed skin is a common sign of food allergies.

What can your Blue French Bulldog be allergic to? Technically, he can develop an allergy to any food he eats but there are some ingredients more likely to trigger food allergies in dogs than others. Some of the most common food allergens for dogs include beef, chicken, dairy, lamb, fish, corn, eggs, wheat, and soy. If you suspect that your Blue Frenchie has a food allergy, you may need to put him on an elimination diet for 12 weeks or until all signs of the allergy have disappeared. At that point you can either keep feeding him the elimination diet or switch to a food that doesn't contain the allergen.

3.) Grooming Requirements for Blue Frenchies

The Blue French Bulldog has a short, smooth coat that is very easy to care for. This breed sheds moderately, so you should plan to brush him a few times a week to keep shedding under control. These dogs do not usually require professional grooming because trimming the coat is unnecessary. If you do not want to bathe or brush your dog yourself, however, you might need a groomer.

When it comes to caring for your dog's coat, use a wire-pin brush or a soft bristle brush to brush him about three times a week. Start at the base of his neck and work your way down his back and sides, always brushing in the direction of hair growth. Next, brush down each leg then have your dog roll over so you can get his belly. The Blue French Bulldog's coat generally isn't long enough to tangle but, if you happen to find a snag, work through it gently with your fingers so you do not hurt your dog.

If your Blue Frenchie is dirty, you can give him a bath but be careful not to bathe him too often or you could dry out his skin. To bathe your dog, simply fill your bathtub with a few inches of lukewarm water and place your dog in it – you can put a bath mat or towel down to keep him from slipping. Then, use a cup or a hand sprayer to wet down your dog's coat and work a little bit of dog-friendly shampoo into a thick lather. Rinse the coat well until you have gotten rid of all of the shampoo suds and then towel your dog dry. Unless your dog gets dirty, you should only plan to bathe him once every 4 to 6 weeks – bathing him too often can dry out his skin and coat.

In addition to brushing your Blue Frenchie's coat, you should also care for his skin folds. If your dog gets wet and the folds of skin do not dry properly, he could develop a bacterial or fungal infection. Make sure to towel-dry your dog after each bath and wipe down the wrinkles on his face and the folds of skin around his shoulders at least once a week. You can purchase wet wipes specifically for this purpose or you can use mild baby wipes.

Caring for your dog's ears is another grooming task you will have to do. Just as your dog's skin can become infected if it stays wet for too long, so can his ears. This is generally not a frequent problem with Blue French Bulldogs because their ears are erect – this allows plenty of air to reach the inner part of the ear. Even so, you want to check your Blue French Bulldog's ears at least once a week. If you smell a foul odor or notice redness or discharge, it could be a sign of infection and you may need to take your dog to the vet.

Aside from cleaning your dog's ears, another grooming task is trimming his nails. Blue French Bulldogs do not tend to be active enough to wear their nails down on their own so you should plan to clip your Blue Frenchie's nails once every week or two. When trimming his nails, be sure to only snip the tip, so you do not accidentally cut off too much and cause your dog to bleed. If you aren't sure how to do it, have a professional groomer show you or ask your veterinarian.

Chapter Six: Blue French Bulldog Training Guide

When you bring home a new dog, training starts right away. Even though your Blue French Bulldog puppy may still be too young to really start learning commands, he will always be watching and learning. When it comes to dog training, there are many different options for training methods, but not all of them are right for your Frenchie. In this chapter, you will receive an overview of dog training methods, as well as specific tips for training your Blue French Bulldog. You will also receive a quick-start guide for housetraining your Blue Frenchie.

1.) Tips for Training Blue French Bulldogs

There are many different training methods out there, but not all of them are right for your Blue French Bulldog. For larger, more dominant breeds, you may need to exercise a firm hand in discipline and authority. For Blue Frenchies, however, they have a friendly temperament and a natural desire to please, so gentle training is recommended. The best type of training for Blue French Bulldogs is positive reinforcement training.

Positive reinforcement training is actually a very simple concept. The idea is that you reward your Blue Frenchie for doing the things you want him to do, effectively reinforcing those behaviors to encourage him to repeat them. For example, if you want to teach your puppy how to sit you would teach him to recognize the verbal command and show him what to do – when he does it, you praise and reward him so he forms a mental connection between the command, the action, and the reward.

Understanding the basics of positive reinforcement training is all you really need. Blue French Bulldogs are intelligent, so they should pick up on new commands quickly as long as you are clear about what you expect and you are consistent in issuing rewards. For the best results when training your Blue Frenchie, you should stick to a daily schedule for feeding, exercise, and training. These dogs thrive on routine and having a set schedule will be very beneficial when it comes time for potty training.

In addition to knowing the basics about positive reinforcement, you should also keep the following Blue French Bulldog training tips in mind:

- Keep your training sessions short – no more than 15 minutes – so your puppy does not get bored.
- Do not rush through things – make sure your puppy understands the desired action before you move to the next command.
- Be consistent about using the same word or command for each action – if you do not use the same word each time, your puppy might get confused.
- Do not become reliant on food rewards – your puppy is highly motivated by food, but giving him a belly rub or a quick walk can also be good rewards.
- Avoid punishing your Blue Frenchie for undesired behaviors – he is unlikely to connect the punishment with the crime and he will just end up fearing you, instead of learning a lesson.

Training takes time but because Blue French Bulldogs are smart, your pup should catch on quick. Keep reading to learn how to potty train your dog.

2.) Frenchie Puppy Crate Training Guide

The best method for housetraining your Blue French Bulldog is called crate training. Basically, you give your puppy many opportunities to do his business outside, so he isn't tempted to do it inside. When you cannot keep an eye on your puppy (such as when you go to work or overnight), you put him in the crate so he does not have an accident. As long as you use the crate for this purpose and you help your puppy form a positive association with the crate, he will not mind being in it. Just do not use it as a form of punishment!

So, how exactly do you go about crate training your puppy? Here's a step-by-step guide:

1. Choose a certain part of your yard where you want your dog to go.
2. Take your puppy outside every hour or so and take him directly to the chosen spot every time.
3. When you take your puppy out, tell him "Go pee" (or choose another command) as soon as you set him down in that area.
4. Wait for your puppy to do his business – if he does, immediately praise him in an excited voice and give him a small treat as a reward.
5. If your Blue Frenchie does not have to go, take him back inside instead of letting him wander around.

6. When you are at home, keep a close eye on your puppy and confine him to whatever room you are in.

7. Watch your Blue Frenchie for signs that he has to go and take him outside immediately if he starts to sniff the ground, walk in circles, or squat.

8. In times when you cannot physically watch your puppy, put him in his crate to reduce the risk of an accident – do not keep any food or water in the crate with him.

9. Let your puppy out immediately before putting him in the crate and after releasing him – you should also take him out after a meal or after a nap.

10. Take away your puppy's food and water about an hour before bedtime until he's able to go the whole night without an accident.

When you first bring your Blue French Bulldog home, you shouldn't expect him to be able to hold his bladder or bowels for more than an hour or two. Even so, you should start crate training right away so he learns good habits from an early age. As he gets older, he'll be able to wait longer – about one hour for each month of age.

3.) Teaching Basic Obedience

Once your Blue Frenchie puppy is old enough, you can start working with him to teach him basic obedience – commands like Sit, Lie Down, Stay, and Come. These things are fairly easy to teach as long as you use positive reinforcement and you are consistent with your commands and your rewards. Keep reading to find step-by-step guides for teaching these four simple commands.

a.) Sit

The "Sit" command is generally the easiest place to start with a new puppy when it comes to obedience training. The command is simple to learn and easy to demonstrate, so your Blue French Bulldog should learn quickly. Here's how you do it:

1. Kneel down in front of your Blue French Bulldog and pinch a small treat between your thumb and forefinger.
2. Get your puppy's attention by waving the treat under his nose until he catches the smell.

3. Hold the treat just in front of your puppy's nose and tell him to "Sit" in a firm but clear voice.
4. Right after saying "Sit," move the treat up and forward toward the back of your puppy's head.
5. Ideally, your puppy will lift his nose to follow the treat and, as he does so, his bottom will lower to the floor – if he does not, try again.
6. As soon as your puppy's bottom hits the floor, tell him "Good sit" and give him the treat.
7. Repeat this training sequence several times, until your puppy responds consistently with the appropriate behavior.

b.) Lie Down

Once your puppy knows how to sit, you can work from there to teach him how to lie down on command. Your puppy will need to have mastered the "Sit" command first, so make sure that he responds consistently when you give him the command. Here's how to teach the "Lie down" command to your puppy:

1. Kneel down in front of your Blue French Bulldog and pinch a small treat between your thumb and forefinger.

Get your puppy's attention by waving the treat under his nose until he catches the smell.

2. Hold the treat just in front of your puppy's nose and tell him to "Sit" in a firm but clear voice.

3. Once your puppy sits, tell him "Good sit" but do not give him the treat yet.

4. Tell your puppy "Lie Down" or "Down" in a clear voice and immediately lower the treat to the floor between your puppy's feet.

5. If your puppy follows the treat and lies down, tell him "Good sit" and give him the treat.

6. Repeat this training sequence several times until your puppy responds consistently with the appropriate behavior.

c.) Stay

Once your puppy knows how to sit on command, you can teach him to stay. Again, he will need to know how to "Sit" properly but once he does, follow this sequence:

1. Start by kneeling in front of your Blue French Bulldog and pinch a small treat in your hand.

2. Hold the treat in front of your puppy's nose so he can smell it then tell him to "Sit".

3. When your puppy sits, give him the "Stay" command and take a quick step backward.

4. If your puppy stays, tell him "Good boy" and step forward to give him the treat.

5. Repeat the sequence, moving back a few more steps each time. As long as your puppy responds consistently, keep rewarding him.

d.) Come

Teaching your puppy to come is fairly easy, but you do need to have a positive relationship with him if it is going to work – your puppy needs to want to come to you. Bribing him with treats will help, but if you are constantly yelling at your Blue French Bulldog outside of training, he may be wary about coming to you when called.

Your puppy will also need to know his name, so you should have worked with him to some degree beforehand to make sure of that. When you are both ready, here is how to teach your puppy to "Come" on command:

1. Start by kneeling in front of your Blue French Bulldog and pinch a small treat between your thumb and forefinger.

2. Hold the treat in front of your puppy's nose so he can smell it then tell him to "Sit".

3. When your puppy sits, give him the "Stay" command and take a quick step backward.

4. Clap your hands and tell your puppy to "Come" in an excited voice.

5. If your puppy comes to you, tell him "Good come" and give him the treat.

6. Repeat this training sequence several times, until your puppy responds consistently with the appropriate behavior.

Once your puppy masters these basic commands, you can work with him to phase out the food rewards. Start by rewarding him every other time he performs well, making sure to keep praising him. Then, you can replace the food rewards with a physical reward like a belly rub or a quick game of tug.

Chapter Seven: Blue French Bulldog Breeding Guide

If one Blue French Bulldog is great, then a whole litter of them must be even better! Right? Maybe not. Breeding dogs is never something you should do on a whim, and it is particularly risky for Blue French Bulldogs and similar breeds. Before you even start to think about breeding your Blue Frenchie, you need to learn the ins and outs of dog breeding. Fortunately, this chapter is full of relevant information! Keep reading to learn the basics as well as more specific information about breeding and raising Blue French Bulldogs.

1.) *Blue French Bulldog Breeding Information*

Before you even consider breeding your Blue French Bulldog, you need to understand the basics about dog breeding. First and foremost, know that carrying and giving birth to a litter of puppies can be stressful for a dog – unless your dog is in excellent health, breeding could be dangerous. You should also know that, even if your dog is healthy, breeding can be tricky for Blue French Bulldogs, because the puppies have such large heads that many dogs experience birthing difficulties.

Aside from the health problems which can result from breeding, breeding your Blue Frenchie also comes with some practical responsibilities. You will need to feed your pregnant dog more than usual and take her to the vet several times during the course of her pregnancy. When she is ready to give birth, you will probably need to have a C-section performed, because natural births are too dangerous. Once the puppies have been born, you will need to feed and care for them as well. Puppies need a lot of vaccines during the first few months, so costs can add up quick.

If, after all of that Blue French Bulldog information you are still interested in breeding yours, you will need to know how dog breeding works. In the same way that human women go through the menstrual cycle, female Blue French Bulldogs go through the estrus cycle, which is also known as heat. This typically happens twice a year, though smaller breeds like the Blue Frenchie sometimes have three cycles per year. In most cases, the first heat cycle will happen around 6 months of age, though some Blue Frenchies may start sooner – around 4 months of age.

Even though your Blue Frenchie may go into heat as early as 6 months, and technically be capable of breeding, she will not be fully mature until 12 to 18 months of age. Many veterinarians recommend waiting until the Blue French Bulldog is 18 months old to breed her for the first time. For male Blue French Bulldogs, they typically go through puberty by 5 or 6 months of age, but they are most fertile after they reach 12 months of age. Recommendations vary, but it is generally best to wait until the dog is 1 year old to breed him with a sexually mature female.

When a female dog starts her heat cycle, you can expect it to last for about 3 weeks on average. The best time to breed your Blue French Bulldog is about 8 to 12 days into her cycle. If the mating is successful, she will become pregnant and go through a gestation period lasting about 63 days, on average. During this time, your dog may start to eat more food but do not go overboard – make sure she is able to eat as much as she needs to, but her food intake should increase slowly in proportion with the weight she gains as the puppies grow and develop.

Blue Frenchies are notoriously difficult to breed so, if your dog does not get pregnant after a few tries, you could try artificial insemination. This process is frequently successful when executed properly, but it can be tricky. The sperm needs to be at a specific temperature and it needs to be inserted directly into the dog's uterus via syringe. You will need to talk to your veterinarian, if this is something you are considering doing.

2.) *Raising Blue French Bulldog Puppies*

If your female Blue French Bulldog becomes pregnant, you should mark the day of conception on the calendar so you can track her gestation period. In most cases, the gestation period will last 60 to 63 days. About a week before your dog's expected due date, you should start watching for signs of labor in case she is early. Blue Frenchies usually stop eating about 24 hours before they give birth and they may also start "nesting" a few days before that.

To limit the mess, make sure your dog has a whelping box lined with newspaper and old towels to keep her comfortable. This is an important stage for female dogs, even if you plan to have a C-section. You will need to schedule the C-section well ahead of time and try to get it as close to the start of labor as possible to minimize complications. Without a C-section, there are certain risks for Blue French Bulldogs – the cervix may not fully dilate, or her uterus could twist and cut off blood flow.

If you are not quite sure whether your dog is in labor or not, you can take her internal temperature. The average internal temperature for a healthy Blue French Bulldog is between 100°F and 102°F (37.7°C to 38.8°C). Once the temperature drops to about 98°F (36.6°C), labor is likely to begin within the hour. You will know that labor is starting when your

Blue French Bulldog begins to show obvious signs of discomfort like pacing, panting, and changing positions. If you have not already taken steps to get your dog to the vet for a C-section, you had best hurry up.

Once the puppies have been born, your female dog will nurse them and care for them. It is important that the puppies nurse as close to birth as possible, because the mother's first milk (called colostrum) is full of antibodies that will help to protect the puppies while their own immune systems develop. The puppies will be completely dependent on their mother's care for a few weeks and they are born with their eyes and ears closed.

Blue French Bulldog puppies usually start to crawl around 7 to 14 days after birth and they are usually capable of walking on their own after 21 days or so. Between 2 and 4 weeks of age, their puppy teeth will start to grow in and they should be fully formed by 8 weeks of age. Around 14 days after birth, the puppies' ears will open and they'll become more active. By three weeks of age, the puppies should be sampling solid food and they should be completely weaned by 8 weeks. When the puppies reach this milestone, they are ready to go to their new homes.

Chapter Eight: Blue French Bulldog Health

As wonderful as they are, Blue French Bulldogs are prone to certain health problems. Many of the conditions to which the breed is prone are related to the breed's shortened facial structure. There are, however, other health problems unrelated to the dog's anatomy. To ensure that your dog stays as healthy as possible for as long as possible, you need to learn everything you can about potential health problems, how to identify them, and how to treat them.

In this chapter, you will find a wealth of health information about the Blue French Bulldog. First, you will receive an overview of some of the most common health problems known to affect the breed including their causes, symptoms, and treatment options. Next, you will receive in-depth information about brachycephalic syndrome and how it might affect your dog. You will also learn about recommended vaccines and you will receive some tips for shopping for pet insurance.

1.) Common Health Problems for Blue French Bulldogs

The Blue French Bulldog has an average lifespan of 11 to 13 years, which is on the shorter end for a small-breed dog. Feeding your pup a high-quality, nutritious diet will help to extend his lifespan, but there are some potential health problems you should be aware of that could shorten your dog's life as well. Here are some of the most common health problems seen in the Blue French Bulldog breed:

- Allergies
- Brachycephalic airway syndrome
- Cataracts
- Cherry eye
- Distichiasis
- Entropion
- Hemivertebrae
- Hip dysplasia
- Intervertebral disc disease
- Patellar luxation
- Von Willebrand Disease

In addition to these breed-specific health problems, you should be aware of some problems that can affect any dog. Heartworm, for example, is a deadly disease that can be transmitted through infected mosquito bites. Fortunately, you can protect your dog with a monthly pill. You will also want to treat your dog with something to prevent fleas and ticks – you can purchase a collar that will do the trick or use a monthly topical application.

Interested in learning more about the ten health problems listed on the previous page? Here's an overview of each (except for brachycephalic airway syndrome, which is covered in the next section).

Allergies

You may be surprised to learn that dogs can suffer from allergies in much the same way that people can. Not only can Blue French Bulldogs develop allergies to certain food ingredients, but they can also develop inhalant or contact allergies. The general signs of allergies in Blue Frenchies include the following:

- Itchy red skin
- Itchy or runny eyes
- Licking the base of the tail
- Sneezing or coughing
- Ear infections
- Diarrhea
- Snoring from throat inflammation
- Chewing the paws

Some of the things Blue Frenchies can be allergic to include grass, weeds, pollen, mold spores, dust, dander, feathers, cigarette smoke, prescription drugs, perfumes, and cleaning products. They can also be allergic to certain flea and tick products, so be very careful which one you choose. You should also never use products on your dog that are not designed specifically for dogs – this includes shampoo.

Cataracts

One of several inherited health problems to which the Blue French Bulldog is prone, cataracts are a condition affecting the eyes. Technically speaking, a cataract is an opacity that forms in the lens of the eye and it can partially or completely obstruct your dog's vision. Though cataracts are not painful, there is a slight risk that the cataract could slip out of place and float around the eye or it could become stuck in the tear duct, blocking fluid drainage.

Unfortunately, cataracts cannot be prevented, especially if it is a condition your puppy inherited genetically. If the cataract is caught while still in the early stages, however, your vet may be able to take steps to slow the progression and maybe even save your dog's vision. In some cases, a dog's vision can be restored by surgically removing the cataract, but there is a fairly long recovery period for this kind of surgery.

Cherry Eye

This condition is common in dogs with large, bulging eyes. Cherry eye is a condition in which the tear gland protrudes from behind the dog's third eyelid, causing a red bulge of tissue to form in the corner of the eye. This condition can be caused by inflammation, infection, or increased pressure in the eye and treatment usually involves treating the underlying cause of the protrusion. If the gland cannot be manipulated into place, surgical removal is an option to keep the problem from recurring.

Distichiasis

This condition is characterized by abnormal hair growth on the dog's eyelids. The hairs grow out of the dog's oil glands in places where eyelashes do not normally grow. As a result, the irritation can cause conjunctivitis, redness, excessive blinking, and excess tear production. Because this condition is very uncomfortable, prompt treatment is required – it could also lead to blindness.

There are actually several kinds of eyelash disorders in dogs that could affect your Blue Frenchie. Trichiasis involves the abnormal twitching of the eyelid along with excess tears and swelling. Distichiasis, in addition to inflammation and redness, can also involve twitching of the eyelid or even a change in iris pigmentation. Treatment usually involves removing the excess hairs by first freezing them with liquid nitrogen and then removing them individually.

Entropion

Another eye problem common in Blue Frenchies, entropion occurs when one or both eyelids rotates inward, causing the eyelashes to scratch the dog's eye. This condition can cause pain and inflammation in the eye as well as excessive tearing. If the condition does not resolve on its own, or if it recurs frequently, surgical correction may be needed to remove the excess eyelid tissue.

In small-breed dogs like the Blue French Bulldog, symptoms for entropion usually include excessive tearing and inflammation. You are unlikely to see mucus or pus discharge from the corner of the eye, like you might in larger breeds. In many cases, the cause of entropion in Blue Frenchies has to do with the shortened facial structure and the shape of the nose. It can also be related to frequent eye infections or other eye irritants. Diagnosis is fortunately fairly straightforward, and treatment usually involves medicated eye drops to reduce the inflammation and to manage the pain.

Heartworm

Though this disease is not included in the list of conditions that commonly affect the Blue French Bulldog, it is one every dog owner should be aware of, because it can affect any dog. Heartworm is a parasitic roundworm that can be transmitted to your dog through the bite of an infected mosquito. If a mosquito feeds on an animal that has adult heartworms, it will take up some of the eggs along with the blood. When the mosquito bites another animal, the eggs will be deposited with the blood, and they will develop into larvae and then travel to the heart where they mature.

In the early stages of heartworm, dogs typically show no symptoms – by the time symptoms emerge, the infection is likely to be quite severe. Signs of heartworm in dogs may include a mild persistent cough, fatigue, reduced appetite, and weight loss. It is recommended that puppies be started on heartworm prevention as early as possible, though they should be tested at 6 months and then six months later just to be sure. Prevention is as simple as giving your Blue Frenchie a pill once a month, so do not neglect it.

Hemivertebrae

Blue French Bulldogs have short tails that can sometimes develop abnormally. Hemivertebrae is a congenital defect in which the vertebrae fuse together or form in an abnormal wedge shape. This can sometimes give the dog a "screw tail" or it could be a serious problem that causes compression of the spinal cord. Weakness in the hind limbs, loss of bladder control, and pain are the common signs of hemivertebrae. It usually does not need to be treated, though anti-inflammatory medications may be administered to help with the pain and swelling.

In some cases, hemivertebrae only affects the tail – when that is the case, it is not a medical concern and probably does not need to be treated. When it affects the rest of the spine, however, it may lead to other clinical symptoms that could be dangerous. Hemivertebrae in Blue French Bulldogs is a congenital condition and it is usually easy to diagnose, so do not ignore the signs – have your dog tested if you suspect he is affected.

Hip Dysplasia

A musculoskeletal issue commonly seen in larger breeds, this is a problem affecting the hip joint. Hip dysplasia occurs when the head of the femur or thigh bone slips out of its rightful place in the hip socket. When the bone is out of joint, it can cause the dog to limp or it might cause total limb lameness. Over time, the wear and tear on the joints can lead to painful inflammation, which may necessitate a surgical repair. In more mild cases, other treatment options include pain medications and anti-inflammatories.

Intervertebral Disc Disease (IVDD)

This is a condition of the spine in which the cartilage that cushions the spinal vertebrae herniates – bulges or bursts out of place. With the cushioning gone, the vertebral discs weigh on each other and press against the spinal nerves, causing pain and inflammation. It can get so bad that the dog becomes paralyzed.

The symptoms of IVDD can vary quite a bit from one dog to another and may include the following signs:

- Neck pain or stiffness
- Lowered head
- Back pain or stiffness
- Yelping unexpectedly
- Arched back
- Sensitivity to touch or movement
- Dragging a leg
- Stilted gait
- Loss of coordination

These signs are most likely to be noticed after your Blue Frenchie has engaged in strenuous exercise or has undergone some physical trauma. This condition usually affects dogs between the ages of 3 and 6 years. Treatment often involves managing the pain or surgical correction.

Patellar Luxation

Similar to hip dysplasia, patellar luxation involves a bone slipping out of joint. This condition occurs when the patella or kneecap slips out of place, making it impossible for your Blue Frenchie to use his knee normally. Dogs may exhibit signs such as limping, staggering, or falling and they may experience pain as well. When the patella is out of position, the dog cannot straighten the knee until the quadriceps muscles relax and the patella is able to slide back into place.

Because many dogs do not experience pain except when the patella slips out of place, it can sometimes be tricky to diagnose this condition. The more it happens, however, the more osteoarthritis the dog develops around the joint, which can lead to stiffness and pain. Treatment for patellar luxation usually involves weight loss and pain management or, in severe cases, surgery.

Von Willebrand Disease

A disease of the blood, von Willebrand disease causes Blue French Bulldogs to bleed excessively with even minor injuries. The problem is that the dog lacks a specific protein (von Willebrand factor), which helps the blood to clot. Signs of von Willebrand disease include bleeding gums, skin bruising, vaginal bleeding, blood in the urine, and blood in the feces.

Von Willebrand disease is a genetically inherited disease known as an autosomal trait – this means that it affects males and females at the same rate. Diagnosis of the disease involves physical exam and medical history, as well as a blood chemical profile. Treatment usually involves a transfusion of whole blood.

2.) *A Word About Brachycephalic Breeds*

The word "brachycephalic" is just a fancy way of saying that a dog has a short nose. Aside from the Blue French Bulldog, other breeds that have a shortened facial structure include Pugs, Boston Terriers, and Pekingese. Though their short noses make these breeds what they are, they also predispose the dog to certain health problems related to something called brachycephalic airway syndrome. But what exactly does that mean?

Brachycephalic airway syndrome is not a disease, but rather a set of anatomical abnormalities which can impact your dog's breathing. The four abnormalities grouped under this heading are:

- Stenotic nares
- Elongated soft palate
- Hypoplastic trachea
- Everted laryngeal saccules

Stenotic nares are simple narrow nostrils that make it difficult for the dog to take in enough air through the nose – this is part of the reason why Blue French Bulldogs tend to pant even when it is not hot out. An elongated soft palate is simply extra tissue in the back of the throat that can relax into the airway, causing a partial obstruction. This is part of the reason why Blue French Bulldogs tend to snore. A hypoplastic trachea is characterized by a trachea that is smaller in diameter than normal and everted laryngeal saccules are simply tiny air sacs that can be sucked into the airway, causing an obstruction.

On its own, brachycephalic airway syndrome is not dangerous or life-threatening. The anatomical abnormalities can, however, affect your dog's breathing which can lead to a dangerous situation. For example, if your dog cannot take in enough air he might be more likely to overheat during the summer and he is less tolerant of vigorous exercise than other breeds. You will need to talk to your vet to determine whether your Blue Frenchie needs to have any of these abnormalities corrected.

3.) *Blue Frenchie Vaccinations and Preventive Care*

Even if your Blue French Bulldog seems to be in good health, you should still take him to the vet once or twice a year for a checkup. Dogs have a natural instinct to hide their pain so, even if your dog is sick, he might not make it obvious to you. If your dog develops a change in behavior without an obvious cause, you might want to take him to the vet just to be safe.

In addition to taking your dog to the vet when he gets sick, you will also need to make sure that he gets certain vaccinations. These vaccines will protect him from common diseases and, once he gets his puppy shots, he'll only need a few of them each year. Here is a quick overview of the different vaccines your dog will need and when:

Vaccination Schedule for Blue French Bulldogs			
Vaccine	**Doses**	**Age**	**Booster**
Rabies (US only)	1	12 weeks	annual
Distemper	3	6-16 weeks	3 years
Parvovirus	3	6-16 weeks	3 years
Adenovirus	3	6-16 weeks	3 years
Parainfluenza	3	6 weeks, 12-14 weeks	3 years

Bordetella	1	6 weeks	annual
Lyme Disease	2	9, 13-14 weeks	annual
Leptospirosis	2	12 and 16 weeks	annual
Canine Influenza	2	6-8, 8-12 weeks	annual

In addition to the vaccines on this list, your vet may recommend others depending where you live. Be sure to ask your vet which vaccines your dog needs and when, so you can stay up to date and bring him back to the office on time for his next round of shots.

4). Should You Consider Pet Insurance?

Because caring for a Blue French Bulldog can be expensive, you may be looking for ways to save some money. One option is to purchase a pet insurance plan. Pet insurance is similar to health insurance for people, but there are some key differences. For one thing, this type of insurance requires you to pay for the costs upfront and then submit a request for reimbursement. The types of costs and the amount covered will vary by plan, so be sure to do your research before you choose a plan.

To purchase a pet insurance plan, you will need to pay a monthly premium – this is just the cost you pay once a month in exchange for coverage. Some companies offer a discount for paying for the whole year up front, so that's something to think about as well. In addition to your monthly premium, most plans also have a deductible – a minimum amount you are responsible for before the plan will start reimbursing expenses. Generally speaking, plans with higher premiums have lower deductibles and vice versa.

When shopping for pet insurance, you should be aware that there are several different types. Most pet insurance plans do not cover preventive care – things like routine vaccinations and spay/neuter surgery. If you want help with these costs, you will have to purchase a specific plan for your Blue French Bulldog puppy. Outside of preventive care, pet insurance plans usually offer coverage for either accidents or illnesses. Each plan comes with specific limitations as to what is covered and how much the plan will pay out, so read the fine print!

In addition to understanding what your plan does and does not cover, you should also be mindful of per-incident or per-year deductibles. Some plans have a set deductible for the year, while others require you to pay a certain amount for each incident. When considering pet insurance for your Blue French Bulldog, think about the health problems discussed earlier in this chapter to determine whether it is worth the cost to you or not.

Chapter Nine: Tips for Showing Blue French Bulldogs

The French Bulldog is a wonderful breed and they generally perform very well in the show ring. Unfortunately, most breed clubs do not accept the Blue French Bulldog for show. That does not mean, however, that you cannot still find opportunities to show your dog! You may have to look a little harder, but the opportunities are out there. In this chapter, you will learn about the breed standard for the Frenchie and you will receive tips for preparing and showing your dog.

1.) French Bulldog Breed Standard

The French Bulldog is an incredibly popular breed, both in the United States and outside of it. This being the case, the breed is recognized by a number of different clubs and breed organizations. In the United States, the Frenchie is recognized by the following organizations:

- American Canine Association (ACA)
- American Canine Registry (ACR)
- American Kennel Club (AKC)
- American Pet Registry, Inc. (APRI)
- Dog Registry of America (DRA)
- French Bulldog Club of America (FBDCA)
- North American Purebred Registry, Inc. (NAPR)
- National Kennel Club (NKC)
- United Kennel Club (UKC)

In addition to these organizations, there are some smaller regional clubs dedicated to the French Bulldog breed. The largest organizations by far, however, are the American Kennel Club and the United Kennel Club. One thing you need to be aware of, however, is that while both of these clubs accept the French Bulldog breed, neither of them accepts the blue coloration.

Outside of the United States, the French Bulldog is recognized by a number of breed organizations. In the United Kingdom, it is recognized by The Kennel Club. Though the Kennel Club does not allow Blue French Bulldogs to be shown, you can still register your dog with the club, as long as it is a purebred. Internationally, the breed is recognized by the Fédération Cynologique Internationale (FCI), or the World Canine Association.

Taking a look at the breed standard for various organizations may help you to understand what an ideal specimen of the Blue French Bulldog breed would look like. You will find a summary of several breed standards in the following pages.

a.) AKC French Bulldog Breed Standard

Appearance and Temperament

The AKC describes the French Bulldog as an active, intelligent, and muscular breed of heavy bone with a smooth coat and a compact build. Weight should not exceed 28 pounds and the proportion should be well balanced. The temperament is adaptable, well-behaved, and affectionate with an even disposition.

Head and Face

The head is large and square with dark, wideset eyes. The ears are known as the "bat ears", being broad at the base and rounded at the tip. The skull is flat between the ears with a slightly rounded forehead. The muzzle is broad and deep with a well-defined stop forming a hollow groove with wrinkles forming a soft roll over the nose.

Body, Legs, and Tail

The neck is thick and well arched, the back strong and short. The shoulders are broad, the body well rounded, and the chest deep and full. The tail may be either straight or screwed while also being short with a thick root and fine tip. The legs are short and muscular, set wide apart.

Coat and Color

The coat is moderately fine, short in length, and smooth in texture. The skin is soft and loose, particularly around the head and shoulders, forming deep wrinkles. Acceptable colors include fawn, white, and brindle as well as brindle and white as well as other colors that do not constitute disqualification.

Faults and Disqualifications

Any alteration aside from the removal of dew claws. A nose color other than black except in light-colored dogs or anything other than bat ears. Color disqualifications include solid black, mouse, liver, black and tan, black and white, and white and black.

b.) United Kennel Club Breed Standard

Appearance and Temperament

The French Bulldog is an active, intelligent, and powerful dog despite its small size. It has a short, compact structure with good bones and a short, smooth coat. The breed is affectionate and sociable by nature as well as lively and playful without being boisterous.

Head and Face

The head is strong, broad, and square with skin that forms nearly symmetrical wrinkles and folds on the face. The skull is flat between the ears with a slightly rounded forehead and a well-defined stop. The muzzle is proportionally short in comparison to the dog's size as well as being broad, deep, and well laid back. The eyes are round and dark, set low and wide apart in the skull. The rims are black and the expression lively.

Body, Legs, and Tail

The body is compact but broad and deep through the chest with a barrel-shaped rib cage. The loin is short but broad, the topline rising progressively from a slight fall behind the shoulders. There is a moderate tuck and a short tail that is thick at the root with a fine tip. The legs are short and thick with visible musculature. The weight should be between 18 and 28 pounds (8 – 13kg).

Coat and Color

The coat is short, smooth, and glossy with a soft texture. Acceptable colors include fawn, cream, white, and brindle as well as brindle and white and any other color besides black and tan, liver, or mouse gray.

Faults and Disqualifications

Faults include heavy face wrinkles that affect breathing or obstruct vision, as well as a muzzle that is too short. Disqualifications include extreme shyness or viciousness, albinism, cropped ears, ears not carried erect, docked tail, and eyes of two colors. Disqualifying colors include black and tan, liver, and mouse gray.

c.) The Kennel Club Breed Standard

Appearance and Temperament

The breed is sturdy, compact, and solid but with good bone and a short, smooth coat. The dog is full of courage, yet with some clown-like qualities as well as bat ears and a short tail. The temperament is vivacious, intelligent, and affectionate.

Head and Face

The head is square in appearance and proportionate to the dog's size. The skull is nearly flat between the ears with a slightly domed forehead and wrinkling on the face. The muzzle is broad, deep, and set back with a well-defined stop and a square jaw. The eyes are dark, round and of moderate size, showing no white when looking straight forward. The ears are medium in size bat ears, being broad at the base and rounded at the tip.

Body, Legs, and Tail

The body is cobby and muscular with well sprung ribs and a gently roached back. The hindquarters are strong and muscular, the feet small and compact. The tail is undocked yet short, as well as low set and thick at the root tapering to a point at the tip. The gait is free and flowing. The ideal size is up to 24 pounds (11 kg) for females and up to 28 pounds (12.5 kg) for males.

Coat and Color

The coat is short and close with a smooth, fine texture and a nice luster. The only acceptable colors are brindle, fawn and pied. Undesirable colors include solid black, black and tan, black and white, mouse, blue, liver, and any pattern of these colors.

2.) Tips for Showing Your Dog

Although the Blue French Bulldog is not eligible for show with the major breed clubs, there are plenty of other registries through which you may be able to show your dog. Keep in mind that each organization and every show will have its own unique set of standards and requirements. Even so, there are a few basic requirements your Blue Frenchie should meet before you enter him in a show.

Here are some general requirements your dog should meet before you start prepping him for a show:

- He should be at least 12 months old (unless the show allows a puppy class).
- He should be fully housetrained.
- He should be properly socialized and have basic obedience skills.
- He should be up to date on all shots.
- He should be a good example of the breed, according to the breed standard used by the show.
- His coat should be clean and well groomed.
- His nails should be properly trimmed.

As long as your Blue French Bulldog meets these basic requirements, you can move forward to learning about the specific requirements for the show you plan to enter him in. Read through the requirements very carefully to make sure your dog does not have any faults or disqualifications – the last thing you want to do is pay to enter your dog in a show just to have him disqualified on a technicality.

When the time for the show comes, you will need to pack up all the supplies you are likely to need for the day. Here is a quick list to use as a reference:

- Your dog's registration and license information
- Proof of rabies vaccine (only in the U.S.)
- A crate or exercise pen to contain your dog
- Grooming supplies and a grooming table (if needed)
- Food, treats, and water for the whole day
- Toys to keep your dog busy
- Cleaning supplies (paper towels, waste bags, etc.)
- A change of clothes, just in case

When the day of the show arrives, make sure you have all of the necessary documentation and get there early – you want to have enough time to get settled in and to take care of any last-minute grooming needs. As you wait for the show to begin, take the opportunity to talk and network with other dog owners – you never know what kind of connections you might be able to make!

During the show itself, pay close attention and follow all rules and regulations. For your first show, keep in mind that there is a bit of a learning curve – do not be discouraged if your dog does not do well the first time around. Take each show as an opportunity to learn and hone your skills, so your dog can keep progressing with each subsequent show. And do not forget to have fun!

Chapter Ten: Blue French Bulldog Facts and Care Sheet

By now you should have a thorough understanding not only of the French Bulldog breed, but of the Blue French Bulldog in particular. The goal of this book is to answer all of your questions and to prepare you to be the best dog owner you can be. Even after reading this book, however, you may have some questions. You may also find that when you actually bring your puppy home, you need to reference some basic facts.

Rather than skimming through the entire book to find the answers to your questions, flip to this chapter to find detailed Blue French Bulldog facts as well as a care sheet for feeding, breeding, and more. Simply scan through the appropriate list of facts to find the information you need. It is as easy as that!

1.) Blue French Bulldog Facts

Breed Size: small

Height: 11 to 12 inches (28 to 30.5 cm)

Weight: 16 to 28 pounds (7.25 to 12.7 kg)

Coat Length: short

Coat Texture: fine and smooth; skin is soft and loose with wrinkles on the face, head, and shoulders

Eyes and Nose: eyes are dark and wideset; nose is black

Ears: broad at the base, round top (bat ear); carried erect

Tail: short and either straight or screwed

Temperament: loving, playful, smart, clownish, lively

Strangers: quick to make friends, not inherently suspicious

Other Dogs: generally dog friendly

Other Pets: low prey drive

Training: smart with a strong desire to please; positive reinforcement training works well

Exercise Needs: moderately low; brisk daily walk

Health Conditions: hip dysplasia, allergies, patellar luxation, intervertebral disc disease, von Willebrand's disease, elongated soft palate, and brachycephalic syndrome

Lifespan: average 11 to 13 years

2.) *Blue French Bulldog Care Guide*

Space Requirements: low; adaptable to apartments/flats

Energy Level: low to moderate

Attention Needs: high; very people-oriented, shouldn't be left alone for long periods of time

Exercise Requirements: average; daily walk plus active playtime is sufficient

Crate: highly recommended, line with a comfy blanket or plush dog bed, size small

Toys: provide an assortment including chew toys as well as interactive/puzzle toys

Confinement: use a puppy playpen or a small spare room when you cannot physical supervise your puppy

Food/Water Bowls: small, stainless steel or ceramic

Shedding Level: low to moderate

Grooming: brush several times a week; use a wire-pin brush or bristle brush

Trimming: unnecessary

Bathing: as needed, no more than every two weeks; bathing too frequently can dry out the dog's skin

Cleaning Ears: as needed, check at least once a week; use dog-friendly ear cleaning solution and cotton balls

Trimming Nails: once a week; trim the minimal amount needed to prevent overgrowth

3.) Blue French Bulldog Feeding Guide

Diet Type: carnivorous

Primary Nutrients: protein, fat, carbohydrates, water, vitamins, and minerals

Protein: supports growth and development in puppies, maintains lean muscle mass in adults

Fat: most concentrated source of energy; best from animal sources like chicken fat and salmon oil

Carbohydrate: amount should be limited; best from digestible sources like whole grains (brown rice and oatmeal) or gluten-free sources (potatoes, peas, sweet potatoes)

Minimum Requirements (Puppy): 22% protein, 8% fat

Minimum Requirements (Adult): 18% protein, 5% fat

Ideal Range (Puppy): 22% to 32% protein, 10% to 25% fat

Ideal Range (Adult): 30% protein, up to 20% fat

Beneficial Additives: dried fermentation products, chelated minerals, vitamin supplements

Calorie Needs: about 600 to 1000 calories daily, varies by size, age, and activity level; average 40 calories per pound bodyweight

Meals per Day: two or three

Feeding Tips: choose a formula designed for small-breed dogs and feed several small meals per day

4.) Blue French Bulldog Breeding Guide

Age of First Heat: around 6 months (some by 4 months)

Breeding Age (male): no younger than 12 months

Breeding Age (female): no younger than 18 months

Heat (Estrus) Cycle: 14 to 21 days

Heat Cycle Frequency: average twice a year, up to 3 cycles per year

Greatest Fertility: 8 to 12 days into the cycle

Gestation Period: average 60 to 63 days

Pregnancy Detection: possible after 21 days, best to wait 28 days before exam

Feeding Pregnant Dogs: increase portion size in proportion with weight gain

Whelping: should be born by C-section

Puppies: born with eyes and ears closed, completely dependent on mother; sleep and nurse all day

Puppy Development: crawling day 7 to 14, walking by day 21, sampling solid food at week 3, weaned by week 8

Litter Size: average 2 to 5, up to 8 per litter

Chapter Eleven: Relevant Websites

After reading through this entire book, you should have a thorough understanding of the Blue French Bulldog and what he is like as a pet. These dogs are friendly and fun-loving, making them a wonderful addition to any family! As you get ready to open your home to a Blue Frenchie, you may find that you need more information about the breed or that you need help finding certain supplies. In this chapter, you will find a list of resources for everything from breed information to dog food, toys, supplies, and more.

1.) *Blue French Bulldog Breed Information*

United States Websites:

Dogtime.
<http://www.dogtime.com>

Vetstreet.

<http://www.vetstreet.com>

American Kennel Club.

<http://www.akc.org>

United Kennel Club.

<https://www.ukcdogs.com>

United Kingdom Websites:

Pets4Homes.

<https://www.pets4homes.co.uk>

French Bulldog Club of England.

<http://www.frenchbulldogclubofengland.org.uk>

The Kennel Club UK

<https://www.thekennelclub.org.uk>

2.) *Blue French Bulldog Food and Treats*

United States Websites:

Chewy.

<https://www.chewy.com>

Petflow.

<https://www.petflow.com>

Pet Supplies Plus.

 <https://www.petsuppliesplus.com>

United Kingdom Websites:

Monster Pet Supplies.

<https://www.monsterpetsupplies.co.uk>

Pet Planet

<https://www.petplanet.co.uk>

Zooplus.

http://www.zooplus.co.uk/

Pets at Home.

<http://www.petsathome.com>

3.) *Blue French Bulldog Supplies and Accessories*

United States Websites:

Drs. Foster and Smith.

<http://www.drsfostersmith.com>

Petsmart.

<https://www.petsmart.com/dog>

1-800-PetSupplies.

<https://www.petsupplies.com>

Wayfair – Dog Beds.

<https://www.wayfair.com>

United Kingdom Websites:

Pet Supermarket UK.

<https://www.pet-supermarket.co.uk>

Zoo Plus – Dog Supplies and Accessories.

<http://www.zooplus.com>

Monster Pet Supplies – Accessories.

<https://www.monsterpetsupplies.co.uk>

Petshop – Accessories.

< http://petshop.co.uk >

Conclusion

While reading this book, you have learned a great deal about the Blue French Bulldog breed. By now, it should be clear to you that while these are great dogs, they are not necessarily the best choice for everyone. If you have a lot of time to spend with your dog and you do not mind doing some training and a lot of socialization, the Blue Frenchie could very well be a perfect fit.

Blue French Bulldogs are beautiful and unique in many ways. These dogs are fairly small, but they have big personalities and yours is sure to take up a lot of space in your heart. This breed loves to spend time with people and is capable of forming close bonds with his owners. Though you should always take your dog for a daily walk, your Blue Frenchie will be more than happy to spend the rest of the day lazing on the couch with you or cuddled up in bed. He also will never say no to play time.

Before you bring home your new Blue French Bulldog puppy, think long and hard about it. It is easy to get caught up in the excitement of getting a new puppy, but you must consider the practical aspects of the decision as well. While Blue Frenchies do not live as long as some other dogs, it could still be a 10- or 12-year commitment. Factor in the commitment of time and finances that it takes to be a good dog owner and ask yourself if it is the right choice.

If you are certain that the Blue Frenchie is right for you, congratulations! You are about to become the proud new owner of a wonderful friend and companion. Whether you choose to buy a puppy from a Blue French Bulldog breeder or you choose to adopt an adult dog, your life is never going to be the same. You will always have someone excitedly greeting you when you get home and someone to watch movies with you on the couch. And you will have an unlimited supply of unconditional love.

When you are ready to bring your new puppy home, be sure to review the information in this book to make sure that your home and your family are ready. Take the time to carefully puppy-proof your home and pick out a spot in the yard that will become your puppy's potty spot. Stock up on chew toys and start shopping for dog food, so that you will be ready when your puppy comes home. And be prepared to spend lots of time cuddling him!

There is no denying the charm of the Blue French Bulldog breed. If you are looking for a friendly, fun-loving, and adaptable breed, look no further. The Blue French Bulldog is perfect – there are no bones about it!

Index

C

D

G

H

I

L

M

N

O

P

Q

R

S

T

References

"10 Things You Didn't Know About the Blue French Bulldog."
Puppy Toob. <http://puppytoob.com>

"Best Food for French Bulldogs: Help Your Frenchie Reach His
Puppy Potential." Here Pup. <https://herepup.com>

"Brachycephalic Airway Syndrome in Dogs." VCA.
<https://vcahospitals.com >

"Breeding Bulldogs and Raising Bulldog Pups." Bulldog DVM.
<http://www.bulldogdvm.com >

"Breeding Your Frenchie." French Bulldogs Matter.
<http://frenchbulldogsmatter.blogspot.com >

Buzhardt, Lynn. "Genetics Basics – Coat Color Genetics in Dogs."
VCA. <https://vcahospitals.com >

Duve, Jay. "What You Need to Know About Feeding Your
French Bulldog." PetHelpful. <https://pethelpful.com/ >

"French Bulldog." Dog Breed Info.
<https://www.dogbreedinfo.com >

"French Bulldog." Dogtime.com. <http://dogtime.com>

"French Bulldog." The Kennel Club.
<https://www.thekennelclub.org.uk>

"French Bulldog." United Kennel Club.
<https://www.ukcdogs.com >

"French Bulldog." Vetstreet. <http://www.vetstreet.com>

"French Bulldog Coat Color Genetics." Puppy Love Ranch.
<http://www.puppyloveneverfails.com >

"French Bulldog – Temperament and Personality." Petwave.
<http://www.petwave.com>

"French Bulldog – Breed and Grooming Tips." Espree.
<https://www.espree.com>

"French Bulldog Diet and Nutrition." Vanilla Flowers.
<http://www.frenchbulldogbreed.net >

"French Bulldog Puppy Training Tips." VetInfo.
<https://www.vetinfo.com >

"French Bulldog Temperament – What's Good About 'Em,
What's Bad About 'Em." Your Purebred Puppy.
<http://www.yourpurebredpuppy.com >

"French Bulldog Training Tips." Canna-Pet. <https://canna-
pet.com>

"Grooming a French Bulldog for the Show Ring." PetCareRx.
<https://www.petcarerx.com>

"Heartworm in Dogs." American Heartworm Society.
<https://www.heartwormsociety.org >

Hillestad, Katharine. "Puppy Proofing Your Home."
PetEducation. <http://www.peteducation.com>

"How to Feed a French Bulldog." PetCareRx. <https://www.petcarerx.com>

"How to Potty Train Your French Bulldog." Vanilla Flowers. <http://www.frenchbulldogbreed.netl

"How to Train a French Bulldog Puppy." The French Bulldog Guide. <http://thefrenchbulldogguide.com>

"Important French Bulldog Nutrition Facts." Shrink-a-Bulls. <http://www.shrinkabulls.com >

Johnson, Jordan. "French Bulldog Breeding – Can I Do It?" All About Frenchies. <http://allaboutfrenchies.com/ >

McNamara, Melissa. "How to Potty Train a French Bulldog." The Nest Pets. < https://pets.thenest.com >

Miller, Mary Beth. "17 French Bulldog Health Issues You Have to Know About." PawedIn. <https://blog.pawedin.com>

"Official Standard of the French Bulldog." American Kennel Club. <http://images.akc.org>

"Puppy Proofing Checklist." PetMD. <http://www.petmd.com >

Sanderson, Sherry Lynn. "Nutritional Requirements and Related Diseases of Small Animals." Merck Manual. <http://www.merckvetmanual.com >

"Training French Bulldogs." Your Purebred Puppy. <http://www.yourpurebredpuppy.com >

"Understanding French Bulldog Colors." French Bullevard. <https://frenchbullevard.com>

"What Colors and Color Patterns Do Frenchies Come In?" BlueHaven French Bulldogs. <http://bluehavenfrenchbulldogs>

"Whelping, Breeding, False Pregnancy and Estrus in Bulldog Bitches." Bulldogs World. <http://www.bulldogsworld.com>

CPSIA information can be obtained
at www.ICGtesting.com
Printed in the USA
LVHW050040200820
663575LV00003B/158